THE BIBLE

A PERSONAL BIBLE STUDY GUIDE

THE BIBLE

by

ALFRED *and* DOROTHY MARTIN

MOODY PRESS

CHICAGO

ISBN: 0-8024-1101-0

Eighth Printing, 1978

Printed in the United States of America

Contents

A Word at the Beginning

The sophistication and depravity of our day are nowhere more clearly seen than in the material that fills bookshelves and finds advertising space in newspapers. Book titles are provocative, magazine covers blatantly suggestive. In defense of this it is argued that life should be shown as it is without the covering of prudery or false modesty. There is continual pressure for less censorship over what is published; however, laws cannot possibly control the thoughts that spring from the evil human heart and find expression as "literature."

Often what is professed to be reality is actually a sham and a perversion. It is not life as it should and could be lived. The Bible gives the only true picture of life, for it alone portrays the One who *is* life—Jesus Christ.

Christians need to be thoroughly grounded in the Word. We need a knowledge of its factual content, its history, its preservation. The certainty that the Bible came from God by inspiration and that it is infallible and inerrant should be a part of our deepest convictions. A settled belief in God's Word will be a source of stability in an uncertain world; it will be a shield against the pressures of life; it will give a reason for the hope that is in us; and it will give us courage to hold forth the Word of life to others.

1

Basic Facts About the Bible

Something for You to Study

There is no other book like the Bible. It is different from every other book because it is the Word of God. This study begins with this basic fact that the Bible is God's Word. However, unlike some facts, this one cannot be proved like a problem in math. There are many things in life which can't be completely explained or understood, and yet we accept them because it would be foolish not to. For example, electricity works whether we understand the principle behind it or not.

We believe the Bible to be God's Word even though we do not fully understand *how* it is. It must be accepted by faith. Yet there is a solid basis of fact for believing the Bible to be the Word of God. There is ample proof that the Bible is what it claims to be—God's Word given supernaturally to man. The most important reason for accepting the Bible as God's Word is the statement of God Himself in 2 Timothy 3:16*a*: "All scripture is given by inspiration of God."

But there are other reasons which can be given to support this belief. These proofs will help you explain your faith in the Bible to other people.

THERE ARE EXTERNAL PROOFS

1. The people who lived at the time the books were written believed they were from God. People in Old Testament times believed that God spoke to them through Moses, Samuel, David, Jeremiah and others. They accepted the messages of these men as coming directly from God. The Jewish nation in the time of Christ believed the Old Testament Scriptures to be God's Word.

2. The Lord Jesus made it clear that He accepted the Old Testament as God's Word (Luke 24:44). He quoted frequently from the Psalms, Daniel, Isaiah, Hosea, Jonah, Zechariah, and other Old Testament books. This indicates that the Old Testament text had been accurately preserved down to His time. Jesus Christ, God, knew whereof He spoke when He gave His stamp of approval to the authority of the Old Testament.

3. When the church was formed after Christ's death, Christians read the Old Testament Scriptures and added the gospels and the epistles as they were written, believing them to be God's Word.

4. Some of the famous authors of the first centuries after Christ—Ignatius, Justin Martyr, Ireneaus—quoted from the Bible in their writings and showed that they believed it to be God's Word.

5. The Bible has endured through centuries of persecution. No other book has been so hated and attacked through repeated generations. Another lesson will discuss this more fully, but it is mentioned here as an additional proof that the Bible is from God.

6. The Bible changes the lives of those who read and believe it. This is probably one of the hardest facts about the Bible to explain or understand. Yet it is true. Books are educational, entertaining, exciting, challenging, or inspirational. Only the Bible can make one able to be a new person because only it tells the way this can be done—through believing in Jesus Christ. This is positive, though intangible, proof that the Bible is from God.

THERE ARE INTERNAL PROOFS

1. The Bible claims to be the Word of God. It is possible to take the testimony of Scripture about itself because this is one of the basic tests used in judging any literary work. The internal evidence of style, content, and language used in

any writing is accepted in judging its merits. It is impossible to dismiss the Bible's claims about itself. They are constantly repeated throughout its pages. Hundreds of times we read such words as "Thus saith the Lord" and "The word of the Lord came to me saying."

2. Fulfilled prophecy is a strong evidence that the Bible is the Word of God. Many events were foretold long before they happened. Examples of this are Micah 5:2 which gives the birthplace of the Messiah, and Psalm 22 and Isaiah 53 which are prophetic of the death of the Lord Jesus Christ. Hundreds of prophecies were made throughout the Old Testament without collusion of the writers and were fulfilled exactly as predicted. Only someone who knows what will happen in the future can write about it and have it happen just as foretold. The only One who has this knowledge is God and He is the Author of the Bible.

3. Though each individual book has its own theme, the basic message of each is centered in Christ. In the Old Testament the message is *He is coming,* and in the New Testament *He has come.* The book of Revelation especially states clearly the additional news that *He is coming again.*

4. The unusual unity of the Bible is proof of its divine origin. If a group of people were selected at random and told to write, without conferring with each other, their ideas about God, man, life, death—or any subject—there would be wide variation in the results. Yet the writers of the Bible, living at different periods of history, in different countries, with different kinds of education, experience and background, coincide in the message they write. Some were kings, some prophets, priests, fishermen, shepherds. Most of the human writers did not write anything else; they were not literary men. The Bible, begun by one man and completed by another almost sixteen hundred years later with about thirty-five others writing in between, is bound together in a wonderful harmony. This summary chart will help you visualize this information.

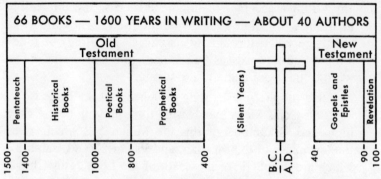

Notice the great span of time over which the Bible was written and the early date for its beginning. Critics used to say that Moses could not have written the Pentateuch, thinking that writing was unknown in his day. But archeological discoveries have shown writing to date back to Abraham's time, five hundred or more years before Moses. The famous code of laws drawn up by Hammurabi, dating from around 2000 B.C., is an example of early writing.

The division of the Bible into chapters and verses was not a part of the original text but was done for convenience much later.

The Old Testament books are divided in subject matter like this:

THE PENTATEUCH (LAW)	HISTORICAL BOOKS	POETICAL BOOKS	PROPHETICAL BOOKS
Genesis	Joshua	Job	Isaiah
Exodus	Judges	Psalms	Jeremiah
Leviticus	Ruth	Proverbs	Lamentations
Numbers	1 and 2 Samuel	Ecclesiastes	Ezekiel
Deuteronomy	1 and 2 Kings	Song of Solomon	Daniel
	1 and 2 Chronicles		Hosea
	Ezra		Joel
	Nehemiah		Amos
	Esther		Obadiah
			Jonah
			Micah
			Nahum
			Habbakuk
			Zephaniah
			Haggai
			Zechariah
			Malachi

The New Testament has these divisions:

HISTORICAL BOOKS	DOCTRINAL AND PRACTICAL BOOKS	PROPHETIC BOOK
Matthew	Romans	Revelation
Mark	1 and 2 Corinthians	
Luke	Galatians	
John	Ephesians	
Acts	Philippians	
	Colossians	
	1 and 2 Thessalonians	
	1 and 2 Timothy	
	Titus	
	Philemon	
	Hebrews	
	James	
	1 and 2 Peter	
	1, 2 and 3 John	
	Jude	

The names of some of the books give the clue to the human writer, though some of the books are anonymous as far as the writer is concerned. But God is the Author of all the sixty-six books in the Bible.

Find Out for Yourself

1. Read 2 Timothy 3:16-17 and note—
    a) who gave the Word. _all scripture inspired by God_
    b) how it was given. _inspired by God_
    c) why it was given. _that man maybe complete & equipped_

What does 2 Peter 1:20-21 add? _no prophecy ever came by impulse of men - men moved by H.S. spoke from God_

What do the words "private interpretation" mean? _mans basic understanding of what is meant_

2. Try this quiz on yourself.

    What is the first chapter of Genesis about? _Creation_

    How many books are there in the Bible? _66_

    Which book has the account of the flood? _Genesis_

Whose life story is told in the gospels? _Jesus_

What group of people is predominant in the Old Testament? _Jews_

When did the church begin? Which book tells of it?

_____

3. Read Hebrews 1:1-2. Which verse fits the Old Testament part of the chart on page 10? _Prophetic_

4. What does the Bible do, according to 2 Timothy 3:15?
   instruct us for salvation thru faith
   _____According to 1 Peter 2:2?
   spiritual milk - grow up to salvation

5. Read Luke 24:27. How does this verse show the unity of the Scriptures? _He interpreted to all the prophets_
   all things in scripture concerning Him

Check Your Memory

Without looking back at the study material answer these questions.

1. The most important reason for believing the Bible is _____

   _____.

2. The two kinds of evidence that the Bible is God's Word are _external_ and _internal_ proofs.

3. One external proof is _____.

4. One internal proof is _____.

5. The span of writing covers _____ years.

6. The theme of the Old Testament is _____;

   the New Testament theme is _____.

7. Can you add the third theme? _____

   Which book especially presents this? _____

Make This Personal

Memorize Psalm 119:9-16.

> Wherewithal shall a young man cleanse his way?
> By taking heed thereto according to thy word.

> With my whole heart have I sought thee:
> O let me not wander from thy commandments.

> Thy word have I hid in mine heart, that
> I might not sin against thee.

> Blessed art thou, O Lord:
> Teach me thy statutes.

> With my lips have I declared all the judgments of thy mouth.

> I have rejoiced in the way of thy testimonies, as much as in all riches.

> I will meditate in thy precepts, and have respect unto thy ways.

> I will delight myself in thy statutes:
> I will not forget thy word.

A Further Word

Christians down through the centuries have pointed to the Bible. The Bible alone, they testify, points unerringly to Jesus Christ as Saviour. The Bible alone is the infallible rule of faith and practice. It alone can speak with the authority of the omniscient God Himself. It alone can tell man what he ought to believe, and what he ought to do. And in it alone can man find full assurance for his faith so that he dares affirm, "I know what I believe."

> Kenneth S. Kantzer, "The Authority of the Bible," in *The Word for This Century,* ed. Merrill C. Tenney, pp. 23-24. Reprinted by permission of the publisher, Oxford University Press, Inc.

2

Where the Bible Came From

Something for You to Study

Since the Bible is God's Word, the natural question to ask is How did we get it? The answer is that God guided the human writers in what was to be written.

Down through the centuries man has generally followed two main methods in his search for truth. One method called empiricism, that knowledge comes only through sensory experience, stresses personal experience. The other, rationalism, only believes in knowledge that is gained through human reasoning. The Bible makes it clear that neither of these methods is adequate to discover truths about God. "Eye hath not seen, nor ear heard" (which eliminates empiricism), "neither have entered into the heart of man" (which rules out human reason) "the things which God hath prepared" (1 Corinthians 2:9) is the Scriptures' declaration of the supernatural realm from which God's truths are learned. The Bible goes on to say "But God hath revealed them unto us by his Spirit" (1 Corinthians 2:10).

Different kinds of material make up the Bible record. *There are historical facts.* Records of events were preserved and handed down verbally and in writing from one generation to another. From such sources, Moses and other writers possibly drew some information about events that happened before their time. Examples of this are the offering of Isaac in Genesis 22; the genealogies in Genesis, Numbers, Chronicles, Matthew and Luke; official documents such as those mentioned in Esther 6:1-2; and Stephen's sermon in Acts 7.

There are accounts of personal experiences. The human

15

writers told of things they saw and heard and did. There are many, many of these firsthand experiences: Moses in Egypt, in the wilderness, receiving the Ten Commandments from God; Daniel in the lions' den; Ezra returning to Palestine; Paul in prison; John on the Isle of Patmos. These were facts they knew about because they had lived them.

There is material directly revealed by God. This is the most important source of all. Through revelation God gave information to the writers which they could not have gotten any other way. No human being could have told Moses about the creation. Only God who was "in the beginning" could have known the details of what happened. The prophecies of Isaiah and Jeremiah, the appearance of Satan before God in Job 1, and the book of Revelation are other examples of directly revealed material.

However, God told the writers what to include whether they wrote by direct revelation, from personal experience, or through the use of historical records.

The question is sometimes asked whether God is giving new revelations to people today and the answer is No. In the Bible, and particularly in the New Testament, God has given His final and complete revelation of Himself and His purposes. This is the meaning of Hebrews 1:1-2. If we believe that the Bible is the Word of God, then we must believe that the Bible *alone* is the Word of God.

The revelation of the Bible and especially of the Old Testament is primarily a revelation of God Himself. It is true that creation reveals God. The Bible itself says that "the heavens declare the glory of God" (Psalm 19:1), but the universe only shows His might and power. This is only a partial revelation. Nature does not reveal all of God's work as the Creator the way Genesis does, nor does it show His supreme love the way the New Testament does.

The Bible gives the only complete record of Jesus Christ. He is spoken of in history books and is recognized as the founder of Christianity, but all the information about Him is found in the Bible. It alone tells who He is and why He came.

There are other subjects we would know nothing about if God did not tell us of them in His Word. The Bible tells about the nation of Israel; it shows how God has worked in human history; it tells of events to come. Only from the Bible can we know about Satan and about the angels. What is found on these subjects in other literature is taken from the Bible revelation but is often sadly distorted. For example, Milton's *Paradise Lost* is the only knowledge some people have of Satan, and it is not biblically accurate.

The Bible alone gives the only explanation of sin and reveals the only way sin can be removed. Almost everyone will admit that sin is present in the world. Where it came from and how to get rid of it are questions that the Bible alone can answer. The problem of human suffering and death have meaning only when seen in the light of God's revelation.

The following chart will give you an overview of the contents of the Bible.

God's Word is true whether it is talking about events in history, about the need for salvation, or about rules for daily living. We can believe it for it is God's revelation of Himself to man.

Find Out for Yourself

1. Read Acts 22:3-11. Compare it with Acts 9:1-9 and Galatians 1:13-24. How are these accounts different?

   _____

   _____Which tells the actual experience as Paul lived it? _____

2. What does Job 38 tell you about God? _____
   _____ **Romans 1:20?** _____

HOW THE BIBLE STORY UNFOLDS

GENERAL BACKGROUND	MAJOR WORLD EMPIRES	PRINCIPAL CHARACTERS AND EVENTS
Early Human History Ends in The Flood		Adam Cain Seth Abel Enoch Noah Ham Shem Japheth
The Chosen Family The Hebrew Race Founded	Egypt	Abraham Isaac Jacob
The Hebrews Become a Nation		The Children of Israel Slavery in Egypt
The Theocracy (Rule of the people by God)		Exodus Under Moses Joshua Conquers Canaan The Judges
The Monarchy (The United Kingdom)		King Saul King David King Solomon
The Kingdom Divided 931 B.C.	Assyria	Judah The Israel Some Good and Prophets All Evil Kings Some Evil Kings
Israel Goes into the Assyrian Captivity 722 B.C.		All Descended Numerous from David Dynasties Apostasy Becomes The Assyrian Prevalent in Judah Captivity
Judah Goes into the Babylonian Captivity 586 B.C.	Babylon	The Babylonian Captivity
The Captivity Ended 539 B.C.	Medo-Persia Greece Rome	A Remnant of Jews Return to Palestine Jerusalem and the Temple Rebuilt
The Birth of Christ 4 B.C.		Christ Comes and Is Rejected
The Church Age		The Day of Pentecost— The Church Is Formed The Gospel Goes Out to the Whole World
Events Connected with the Second Coming of Christ		The Second Coming of Christ

_____ John 3:16? _____

Could you know the facts in Job 38 without having a copy of the Bible? _____ Whàt about the fact in John 3:16? _____

3. Read Luke 1:1-4. Note verse 1 especially. Which of the kinds of Bible material referred to in this lesson would fit the verse? _____ What about verse 2?

4. What does James 1:5 say about the source of wisdom?

Check Your Memory

Without looking back at the study material answer these questions.

1. The two main methods men use to find truth are _____ and _____.

2. The Bible says neither method can be used to discover truth about _____.

3. God's method of making truth known is called _____ _____.

4. The Bible is made up of three kinds of material:

   a) _____

   b) _____

   c) _____

5. Only the Bible gives information about the following subjects:

a) _____

b) _____

c) _____

6. The Bible is primarily a revelation of _____.

Make This Personal

Memorize 1 Corinthians 2:9-12.

But as it is written, eye hath not seen, nor ear heard, neither have entered into the heart of man,
The things which God hath prepared for them that love him.

But God hath revealed them unto us by his Spirit:
For the Spirit searcheth all things, yea, the deep things of God.

For what man knoweth the things of a man, save the spirit of man which is in him?
Even so the things of God knoweth no man, but the Spirit of God.

Now we have received, not the spirit of the world, but the spirit which is of God;
That we might know the things that are freely given to us of God.

A Further Word

So far as human knowledge goes, the Bible deals as freely with things unknown as it does with the known. It speaks with utmost freedom and assurance of things altogether outside the range of human life and experience— of things eternal as well as of time. There is a border beyond which the human mind, basing its conclusions on experience, cannot go; yet the human authors of the Bible do not hesitate when they reach that boundary, but move majestically on into unknown realms with intrepidity. By what other means than through the Bible may one gaze into eternity either backward or forward?

L. S. Chafer, *Systematic Theology*
(Dallas: Dallas Seminary, 1947), 1:27.

3

How God Gave the Bible

Something for You to Study

Two facts we've talked about so far seem to be contradictory. One is that God is the author of the Bible; the other is that it was written by many different men. How can both these facts be true? Probably more controversy has raged around this aspect of the doctrine of the Bible than any other area. Our problem is not to determine what men think is a reasonable theory to account for the Bible; it is to discover what the Bible itself says about its origin.

The answer is that the Bible was given by inspiration. The Bible claims this in 2 Timothy 3:16, where the Greek could be translated "Every scripture is God-breathed." The *fact* of it is stated; the *how* is not. This is a miracle for which there is no explanation. It must be accepted by faith in the God "that cannot lie" (Titus 1:2).

Many questions have been asked about the Bible such as How can we know the human authors didn't make mistakes as they wrote? Are we sure that Moses' record of the Exodus is based on accurate fact? How do we know the account of the life, death and resurrection of Jesus Christ is accurate? These questions and others cannot be ignored. The Bible says that man can be saved only through faith in Jesus Christ. But unless we can be sure the Bible is true, we can't be sure of the momentous matter of our salvation.

VARIOUS THEORIES OF INSPIRATION

1. *Naturalistic.* According to this view the Bible was written by men who were unusually gifted as writers. Like Shake-

speare or Milton or other famous writers, the authors of the Bible had outstanding ability which shows in their writings and which has caused them to endure through the centuries. If this were true, the authors, writing out of their own knowledge, would have made the same mistakes in basic judgments that all human beings make and their writings could not be trusted in eternal matters.

2. *Partial.* The statement most frequently made by those who hold this view is that the Bible *"contains* the Word of God." This would mean that certain parts are inspired and others are not. Moral ideas and principles, yes; genealogies, no. The criterion for judging is the way one feels when he reads it. The individual human reason becomes the authority to judge the truth of what God has said. This makes the authority of the Bible of no value.

3. *Universal.* This is the idea that ordinary Christians today can be just as inspired as were the original human authors. It would then be possible to write a new Bible in any generation, for it would be the writers rather than the writings that are inspired. But the Bible makes it clear that it alone is God's final and complete revelation.

4. *Dictation.* This is the idea that the human authors were merely machines who automatically wrote what God dictated to them. Such a view does not account for the fact that Moses does not write like Paul nor James like Isaiah. There is a great difference in the style of the writers. God worked through the distinct personalities of the men He used.

5. *Dynamic.* According to this view God gave certain concepts to men and let them express them in their own way. But human writers, because they are human, would use words that were inferior to those God would use. We could not be sure that they had chosen the right words to accurately represent God's thoughts.

THE BIBLICAL VIEW OF INSPIRATION

Two words are used in theology to help explain inspiration. One is *verbal,* which means that the very words of the Bible were inspired. Why is this necessary? Couldn't God simply have given the basic ideas He wanted and left the choice of words to the writers? The question can be answered by asking Can you tell what someone is thinking without his telling you in words? Verbal inspiration guided the choice of the words the writers used, while it respected their individual style, characteristics and vocabulary.

The other word is *plenary,* which means that the whole Bible —all of Scripture— is equally inspired by God. Some portions of the Bible may be more beautiful than others; some more important for salvation; some more essential for living a holy life; but it is all equally inspired.

It is important to realize though that verbal plenary inspiration refers only to the original manuscripts as given by God. It does not include the many copyings through which the Bible has gone since it was first given by God.

Notice that there is a difference between revelation and inspiration. Revelation is the *communication* of truth which otherwise could not be known. Inspiration is the *recording* of that truth. Not everything in the Bible was directly revealed but it was all inspired. Notice the sources of biblical material given in the last lesson, and you will see the logic of this.

There are some things in the Bible which are not true. For example, some of the conclusions of Job's friends are not true, but they are truly recorded. Satan's words are not true; he did not speak by God's inspiration. But what he said was accurately set down by the writer of Job under God's inspiration. The statement of the fool in Psalm 14:1 is not true, but it is given as the true feeling of such a person.

There are two additional terms you should be familiar with. One is *inerrant,* meaning that the Bible is free from mistakes. The other is *infallible,* that the Bible is not able to be wrong because it comes from God who is the source of all wisdom

and knowledge. Notice that it is not the writers who are inerrant and infallible but their writings. Think about the importance of these two terms in the light of all that has been
discussed so far. If the Bible had the possibility of error, could
we trust it for those facts we need for eternity? Could we trust
the God who gave it?

Painstaking study by scholars has proven that the small
percentage of mistakes in the Bible is due to errors in copying
and do not affect any doctrine of Scripture.

Unfortunately, whenever there is a difference between the
Bible, which claims to be God's Book, and human books, it is
often assumed that the Bible is wrong. Many people will not
believe the Bible unless some human discovery corroborates
it—as archeology has consistently done in recent years. Men
reject the Bible which has existed for centuries and yet accept without question the statement of a recently unearthed
cuneiform clay tablet. The correct view is to believe the Bible
first and test human knowledge by it.

Is your Bible inspired? Yes and no. The text is inspired but
your actual copy is not. It is a copy and a translation. There
are millions of copies of the Bible, but each is not individually
and separately inspired. It is God's message given in the original manuscripts which is God-breathed, and we have the
privilege of reading this message daily.

Find Out for Yourself

1. Notice the claims of the Old Testament writers to inspiration. Read Exodus 4:10-15. What is Moses' objection in
   verse 10? ———————————— God's answer in verse 12?
   ———————————————————— Read Zechariah
   1:6 and note the prophet's objection to God's call. ———
   ———————————— What is God's resource in verses 7-9?
   ———————————————————— Read Zechariah.

7. Where does the prophet say he got the words he spoke?

_____

2. Notice the claims of the New Testament writers. What is Paul's claim in 1 Corinthians 14:37? _____

_____

Read 2 Peter 3:15-16. What "other scriptures" does Peter mean? _____
What comparison is Peter making between Paul's letters and other Scripture? _____

_____

3. Read Revelation 1:9-11 and 19 and note the writer _____
_____, the speaker _____, and what was to be written _____

_____

Check Your Memory

Without looking back at the study material answer these questions.

1. God, the Author of the Bible, gave it by _____.

2. The two theological terms used to describe the Bible are *verbal* which means _____
and _____, meaning all of Scripture is inspired by God.

3. Explain why a belief in inspiration is necessary if we are to have confidence in the Bible. _____

_____

4. Can you show that the dictation theory of inspiration is
   false? If necessary, use your Bible to cite specific verses.

   _____

   _____

   _____

5. State the difference betwen revelation and inspiration. _____

   _____

   _____

   Can you illustrate it by an example other than that used in
   the text? _____

   _____

Make This Personal

Memorize 2 Timothy 3:14-17.

> But continue thou in the things which thou hast learned and
> hast been assured of,
> Knowing of whom thou hast learned them;
> And that from a child thou hast known the holy scriptures,
> Which are able to make thee wise unto salvation through faith
> which is in Christ Jesus.

> All scripture is given by inspiration of God,
> And is profitable for doctrine, for reproof, for correction, for
> instruction in righteousness:
> That the man of God may be perfect,
> Throughly furnished unto all good works.

A Further Word

Yet the sovereignty of God must always be the background from which Christian theology begins. He is Creator and Lord, and His freedom to reveal Himself if and
as He will must be maintained. He may write His glory

in the stars, and, if He desires, He may inscribe Ten Commandments on stone. If He can create man, the communication to him of ideas and words in man's language is no great burden. If God's Spirit breathed into man the gift of a unique life, qualifying him for an eternal destiny, that same Spirit assuredly can breathe out to sin-ensnared man the redemptive words of God.

Carl F. H. Henry, "Divine Revelation and the Bible," in *Inspiration and Interpretation,* ed.
John F. Walvoord, p. 271. Used by permission of Wm. B. Eerdmans Publishing Co.

4

Why These Sixty-six Books Were Chosen

Something for You to Study

There were other books written about some of the important events that happened during the hundreds of years that are covered by the Old Testament, but they are not part of the Bible. There are others containing stories about the Lord Jesus and His disciples, but they do not make up the Bible either. What rules were used in deciding which books were to be included and which were not?

This is a problem of canonicity. The word *canon* has the idea of a rule or measuring rod. It is used to refer to the tests that determined the choice of the books of the Bible. Two of these tests are as follows:

1. The *authorship* of the book. One of the most important tests concerned the writer. The questions asked were Does he speak with authority? and Is there evidence that he is a spokesman for God? But some of the books were anonymous and yet, although the human authors were unknown, these books were included in the Bible. This leads to the second test.

2. The *content* of the books. There was something about the sixty-six books that made them different from other writings of their times. The men who considered the books that form the Bible could tell which ones were from God just by reading them. For example, there are other books written about the earthly life of the Lord Jesus. But just as one can tell a fairy story from a true biography, so there is a difference between these books and Scripture.

Apocryphal is the word used to describe these books. Fourteen tell the history of the Jewish nation between the close of the Old Testament and the coming of Christ. Some are historical, such as the books of the Maccabees; others are fanciful. The New Testament apocryphal books profess to give more details about the childhood of Christ and more information about the apostles. The material in these was invented by the writer and not given by inspiration of God.

DEVELOPMENT OF THE OLD TESTAMENT CANON

The history of the Old Testament canon can be traced by starting with the books of the law, Genesis through Deuteronomy, which were kept in the ark of the covenant (Deuteronomy 31:24-26) during the journey through the wilderness on the way to the promised land. The books which were written from then until the time of David (about 1000 B.C.) were kept in the temple with the books of law. The prophetical books were kept as they were written, and all were recognized by the people as God's authoritative Word. Unfortunately many of the kings of Israel and Judah were ungodly, and God's Word was ignored.

Then came the destruction of Jerusalem by Nebuchadnezzar and the long Babylonian captivity (605-536 B.C.), and the books were scattered. Some copies were lost and some destroyed. After the return from Babylon, the Scriptures were reassembled and recopied. This happened in the fifth century B.C. under the direction of Ezra and Nehemiah. The canon of the Old Testament closed with the book of Malachi written about four hundred years before Christ. Note this time sequence:

Old Testament ← 400 Silent Years → *New Testament*
   Malachi   Gospels

But the men who formed the canon of the Old Testament did not decide by themselves which books were from God and which were not. They simply gathered together those that were already recognized as being from God. These books had been God's message to His people since the time of Moses. It was evident at the time of Christ that the Jewish nation regarded the books in the Old Testament as Scripture. They are the identical books we have in our copies of the Bible.

DEVELOPMENT OF THE NEW TESTAMENT CANON

The New Testament canon is easier to trace historically since the books were all written within the same century. In spite of this, formation of the canon was a slow process. Because the churches were scattered, and communication and travel facilities were poor, it was difficult to circulate the writings quickly.

This period in the early church was one of intense persecution so that the gospels and the letters of Paul and Peter and other writers had to be hidden to keep them from being destroyed. That they were preserved and read is shown by the numerous quotations from the New Testament that are found in other writings in the first centuries after Christ.

The apostle Paul's letters apparently were assembled first and were in general use by A.D. 100. Then the four gospels, Acts, 1 Peter, and 1 John were added. Finally, 2 and 3 John, 2 Peter, Hebrews, James, Jude, and Revelation were included in the New Testament canon. Some apocryphal material such as the Epistle of Barnabas was read for a time. However, it clearly did not have the ring of apostolic authority and was not included in the canon.

The matter of which books were from God and which were not was not just an academic question to believers in the first and second centuries. It was a matter of vital concern even during the reign of Emperor Diocletian in the third century, for one of the particular aims of his persecution was the destruction of the Bible. It was in reading the Scriptures that Christians found courage to stand in the face of certain death.

The famous church historian Eusebius lived through this period and on into the reign of the Emperor Constantine, who reversed the orders of his predecessor. Constantine asked for fifty copies of the Bible to be delivered to him in Constantinople. It is interesting to note that the books which comprised the New Testament then are exactly those which we have now. These twenty-seven books were formally acknowledged by the Council of Carthage in A.D. 397 and the canon of the Bible was officially accepted.

Remember, however, that the decrees of men settled the question *only* because God already had decreed: "All scripture is given by inspiration of God." The God who guided in the writing of His message so that it would be exact guided also in the selection of which books would form the Bible. The canon did not make the books authoritative; they already had the authority of being God's Word. We don't know how God caused men to write His Word, but we can trace the logical steps He used in helping men to preserve the Word.

QUESTIONS STILL PERSIST

The closing of the canon did not settle forever all debate about the Bible. The authority of the Word of God was the crux of the battle during the Reformation. And it is the point at which departures from the faith are made today. Whenever the Bible as the Word of God is doubted, there is first a falling away from established doctrines and then a corresponding decay in personal living. In these days the Christian must be constantly on guard against the critic of God's Word who, in the name of scholarship, casts doubt upon the genuineness and authority of the Bible.

Find Out for Yourself

1. Read Exodus 13:1; Leviticus 18:1; 1 Chronicles 17:3; Jeremiah 1:9; Ezekiel 15:1; Amos 3:1. What do the verses indicate about the opinion of the writer as to where he got his message? ——————————————————————

Why do you think the men did not take the credit for the message for themselves? Think of several reasons:

_____

_____

_____

2. Which books in the Bible speak most personally to you?

_____

3. What particular need in life would Revelation 21:4 meet?

_____

    Isaiah 40:11? _____

    Psalm 91? _____

    Acts 4:19-20? _____

Check Your Memory

Without looking back at the study material answer these questions.

1. Canonicity refers to the _____.

2. Two of the tests used in fixing the canon were _____ _____ and _____.

3. Two men prominent in forming the Old Testament canon were _____ and _____.

4. Name the chief characteristic of the New Testament apocryphal books. _____

5. The chief aim of the persecution of Diocletian was _____ _____.

6. The Council of _____ in A.D. 397 officially closed the canon of the Bible.

7. State in your own words the basic reason why these particular sixty-six books form the Bible. ⸺⸺⸺⸺⸺⸺⸺⸺

⸺⸺⸺⸺⸺⸺⸺⸺⸺⸺⸺⸺⸺⸺⸺⸺⸺⸺⸺⸺⸺⸺⸺⸺⸺⸺

Make This Personal

Memorize 2 Peter 1:19-21.

We have also a more sure word of prophecy;
Whereunto ye do well that ye take heed, as unto a light that shineth in a dark place,
Until the day dawn, and the day star arise in your hearts:

Knowing this first,
That no prophecy of the scripture is of any private interpretation.

For the prophecy came not in old time by the will of man:
But holy men of God spake as they were moved by the Holy Ghost.

A Further Word

The idea of a canon did not first originate with the early Church, but the community of faith had before it the Old Testament in a unitary form, referred to by Jesus as "the law and the prophets," and appealed to as a canon, in judgment even upon the religious tradition which surrounded it. The Old Testament canon lacked its climax; it ended with promise and anticipation, but halted short of fulfillment. Jesus Himself taught His disciples to look for an enlargement of the canon; He would have somewhat to say to His followers even after His death. The apostles impose their letters authoritatively on the churches in His name, as divinely inspired. This is the spirit in which the writings were received from the very beginning.

Carl F. H. Henry, "Divine Revelation and the Bible,"
in *Inspiration and Interpretation,*
ed. John F. Walvoord, p. 274. Used by permission of Wm. B. Eerdmans Publishing Co.

5

How It Was Kept Through the Centuries

Something for You to Study

People are sometimes surprised to find that the actual originals of the book of Deuteronomy or 1 Kings or Romans or Hebrews, that is, the original handwritten manuscripts, no longer exist. They ask How can we know that we have the Word of God if we have no original documents to prove it?

Many who express this doubt do not question the authenticity of the classics of literature even though none of those original manuscripts exist either. The argument is that the ancient secular writings of Aristotle and others have been too carefully proved to be doubted. But the Bible also has sufficient proof of its genuineness.

HISTORY OF THE COPIES

We have already discovered that inspiration applies only to the original manuscripts. The various copies are *not* separately inspired. Rather, God worked to preserve His Word in the many copies which can be studied and compared for the evidence they give of the original text. The copies and manuscripts have been traced back many centuries.

Printed copies of the Scriptures are kept safely in various countries and date as far back as the middle of the fifteenth century. For example, in the Royal Library in Berlin is a Hebrew copy of the Old Testament dated 1494. It was from this copy that Martin Luther made his German translation. Here is evidence that the Old Testament existed four hundred years ago in the form we now have it.

Manuscripts take us back from the fifteenth to the second century. Many of the manuscripts prior to this time were de-

stroyed during the many persecutions. However, new discoveries are constantly being made which corroborate the authenticity of the Bible. One of the recent confirmations was the
discovery of the Dead Sea Scrolls in 1947 in the Qumran community, which was broken up just before the destruction of
Jerusalem in A.D. 70. Included is a manuscript of Isaiah much
older than other existing Hebrew manuscripts, which confirms
the accuracy of the text in our Bibles.

The Septuagint, the Greek translation of the Old Testament,
dating between 250-150 B.C. gives evidence of the Old Testament text which was the accepted Scripture of the early Christian church.

There are more than four thousand manuscripts of either
part of the Bible or of the entire Bible which are available to
scholars for study. All of them date from the fifteenth century
back toward the time of the original writing. When we realize
that of the works of Homer, one of the famous authors of antiquity, there is not a known complete copy of his work earlier
than A.D. 1300, we see anew the miracle God performed for
His Word.

GOD PRESERVED HIS WORD IN SPITE OF MANY COPYINGS

Before the invention of printing everything was written by
hand. The Hebrew scribes worked very carefully, pronouncing
each word aloud before they wrote it. They carefully wiped
their pens before writing the name of God, so there would be
no fuzz or lint to mar His name on the page. If, in spite of their
care, there was a mistake, they often destroyed the whole page
rather than trying to correct the mistake. Not one word was
copied from memory. The amazing thing is not that there are
copyists' errors, but that there are so few.

While many thousands of variant readings exist, the great
bulk of them pertain to such matters as spelling and word
order which would not alter the meaning of the text. No major
doctrine of Scripture is affected by any apparent errors in
copying. The fact that there are so few mistakes in a book

that was copied and recopied through many centuries is another evidence of the way God has kept His Word safe.

GOD PRESERVED HIS WORD IN SPITE OF MUCH OPPOSITION

Reference has been made already to the severe persecutions of Diocletian. There were many such attempts to stamp out Christianity which would include destroying the Bible. With the invention of printing and the subsequent rapid production of the Bible, the pace of the persecution quickened as more people read the Bible and discovered for themselves liberating truths which the church had kept hidden. Men and women died for the privilege of owning and reading the precious Book. Names like John Huss, Wycliffe, Tyndale, and others will forever endure as monuments to the courage of those who believed the Bible to be the Word of God.

GOD PRESERVED HIS WORD IN SPITE OF MANY TRANSLATIONS

The translators could have destroyed the Bible. As they worked to put the original Hebrew and Greek in various languages, meanings could have been changed, ideas shifted—intentionally or unintentionally—and God's Word destroyed. It wasn't, because God watched over this part of its preservation also. The true inspired text of Scripture has not perished but lies in the manuscripts and is represented so carefully and remarkably in the translations that we need have no fear of missing the voice of God.

Find Out for Yourself

1. What claim is made for God's Word in Psalm 119:89 and

   152? _____

   What does Jesus add in Matthew 24:35? _____

   _____

   What further thought is given in 1 Peter 1:22-23? _____

   _____

2. Read Deuteronomy 31:24-26 and 32:46-47. Compare the
   picture there with the one in 2 Kings 22:8-13. What com-
   mand in Deuteronomy had been ignored by the people?

   _____

   What significance do you see in the fact that the Law of

   God was discovered in His temple? _____

   _____

3. Read Jeremiah 36 and note the purpose of writing _____

   _____,

   where the scroll was first read _____

   _____, the second reading _____

   _____, the king's

   response when it was read to him _____

   _____, and God's response to the

   king's action _____

   _____.

4. Choose any two Bible verses and write them here from
   memory.

   _____

   _____

   _____

   _____

   _____

   _____

   Did you make any mistakes? Would you want to have to

   copy the whole Bible in this way? _____

5. Suppose your Bible were to be taken from you at the end of this month. What would you do to retain some portions of it? _____

Which portions would you especially want to keep? Name them in order of importance to you.

_____

_____

_____

_____

_____

Check Your Memory

Without referring to the study material answer these questions.

1. Inspiration refers only to _____.

2. Printed copies of the Bible date back to the _____ century.

3. The discovery of the _____ has given evidence of the antiquity of Scripture.

4. Two references that indicate the Bible's claim that it will endure forever are _____ and _____.

5. What conclusion can one assume from the fact that there are comparatively few errors in the Bible in spite of the many times the manuscripts were copied? _____

_____

6. How could a translator endanger the Bible text? _____

_____

Make This Personal

Memorize Psalm 119:89-93.

For ever, O LORD,
Thy word is settled in heaven.

Thy faithfulness is unto all generations:
Thou hast established the earth, and it abideth.

They continue this day according to thine ordinances:
For all are thy servants.

Unless thy law had been my delights,
I should then have perished in mine affliction.

I will never forget thy precepts:
For with them thou hast quickened me.

A Further Word

Jehovah's covenant, namely, that His Word will endure forever, has been discharged to the present hour. Men have done what they could to destroy the influence of the Scriptures. They have both testified against them and predicted their subsidence; but at no time in the world's history has the Bible been more a power for good, nor has it ever been more clearly marked off for an ever increasing influence. The preservation of the Scriptures, like the divine care over the writing of them and over the formation of them into the canon, is neither accidental, incidental, nor fortuitous. It is the fulfillment of the divine promise. What God in faithfulness has wrought will be continued until His purpose is accomplished. There is little indeed that men can do to thwart the effectiveness of God's Word, since it is said of that Word, . . . "For ever, O LORD, thy word is settled in heaven" (Psalm 119:89).

L. S. Chafer, *Systematic Theology,* 1:124.

6

From One Language to Another

Something for You to Study

We don't often stop to realize that the Bible from which we read is a book that has been translated from another language. Many books have awkward expressions and sound cumbersome and unnatural when translated from one language to another. Not so the Word of God. A further evidence of its inspiration and preservation by God is the freshness and vitality that fills it regardless of the many translations it has undergone.

The particular emphasis of this lesson is the English Bible and the thrilling story of how it came into existence. The English Bible is based on three sources translators used in their important work.

1. Manuscripts—old copies of the books of the Bible made from the original manuscripts.
2. Versions—either translations from the manuscripts or translations of translations.
3. The fathers—quotations and references to the Scriptures by well-known Christians in the first centuries after Christ. Some of the best known of these are Justin Martyr and Irenaeus in the second century, Origen and Tertullian in the third century, and Eusebius of Caeserea and Jerome in the fourth century.

The Bible used in England was the famous Latin translation, the Vulgate, made by Jerome in A.D. 406. It was of little use to the ordinary person in England who did not know Latin and who could not afford in any case to have his own personal copy of the Bible. The Bible was a closed book to the people in

41

England in these early centuries. A name that comes out of the past in the fascinating history of the English Bible is *Caedmon,* an illiterate stableboy who was employed in a monastery in England. He began to sing the few parts of the Bible that had been translated into English by the monks. These "songs" became so popular that they were written down and used by others. This was not a translation, of course, but God's Word in the ordinary language of the people was beginning to come through. Later a monk known as *Venerable Bede* translated the Gospel of John into English in the eighth century. *King Alfred the Great* in the next century translated parts of the Psalms into English.

But it was *John Wycliffe* in 1380 who gave the people the first Bible in English, basing his translation on the Latin Vulgate. It was not widely circulated because of the length of time required to write out a copy and because the cost was beyond the reach of the people for whom the translation was intended. Wycliffe, though he had to translate in hiding and on the run, died a natural death.

This was not true of some of his successors, one of whom was *William Tyndale.* His translation, the first English New Testament translated directly from the Greek and printed in 1525, was available throughout England. He wanted "the boy that driveth the plow" to know the Scriptures. Though Tyndale was hounded by persecution and eventually strangled and burned at the stake, his dying prayer "Lord, open the King of England's eyes" was answered. His translation of the New Testament which was published in 1534 became the basis for other translations, including the Authorized or King James Version of 1611. The American Standard Version was published in 1901 as a revision of the King James. No matter what modern English translations a person may read, he should have a familiarity with these two if he is to be adequately grounded in the English Bible. The Revised Standard Version New Testament was published in 1946 and the whole Bible in 1952. There have been many translations and paraphrases of the

Bible in recent years. All of this information can be summed up in this way:

Original Manuscripts

↓

Ancient Copies

↓

Ancient Versions

↓

Vulgate—406

↓

Wycliffe—1380

↓

Tyndale—1534

↓

Great Bible—1539

↓

Geneva Bible—1560

↓

King James Version—1611

↓

American Standard Version—1901

↓

Revised Standard Version—1952

↓

MODERN TRANSLATIONS AND PARAPHRASES

The 20th Century New Testament

Williams' New Testament

Good News for Modern Man

New English Bible

The Berkeley Version

The Living Series of Scripture Paraphrases

The basic principle a translator must always follow is to be true to the original meaning of the text. This is difficult at best and sometimes a translator does not adhere very closely to this principle. In an attempt to reach the ear of modern man, a translator may forget that he is handling God's Word, with the result that he gives not God's authoritative Word, but his idea of what God said. Sometimes a translation is not a translation at all but a paraphrase, a running commentary, or an interpretation, which gives not what the writer said, but what the translator thinks he said. This is one reason why comparing versions is helpful.

There are various reasons why new translations of the Bible are constantly being made. One reason is the way the English language has changed over the centuries. As an example of the change, compare these translations of Luke 10:30-33.

The first is from Tyndale's 1534 version:

> A certayne man descended from Hierusalem to Hierico, and fell in to the hondes of theves, which robbed him of his rayment and wounded him, and departed levynge him halfe deed. And by chaunce ther came a certayne preste that same waye, and when he saw him, he passed by. . . . Then a certayne Samaritane, as he iornyed, . . . had compassion on him, and went to and bounde vp his woundes, and poured in oyle and wyne, and put him on his awne beaste, and brought him to a common ynne, and made provision for him.

Now compare the King James Version which reads: "But a certain Samaritan, as he journeyed, came where he was: and when he saw him, he had compassion on him" (v 33).

Here is the same verse in the New Testament in the Language of Today: "Then a Samaritan, as he was traveling, came near him, and when he saw him, he felt sorry for him."

Each translation attempts to reach modern man with the ageless Word of God. God can use any translation which is true to His original Word.

Find Out for Yourself

1. How would you answer someone who said it didn't matter whether or not the translations of the Scripture are accurate? _____

   _____

   _____

2. Read John 3:16. Try putting it into your own words without referring to a modern translation. Did you find it hard to use words other than the King James? If so, why?

   _____

   _____

3. Compare specific portions of Scripture—Genesis 1; Psalm 23; Luke 2; Hebrews 1—in as many different versions as are available to you. Notice the length of the translation; the simplicity of words that are used; any change in meaning; the beauty of the passage; and the ease of memorization.

Check Your Memory

Without looking back at the study material answer these questions.

1. State one evidence this lesson gives that supports the inspiration and preservation of the Bible. _____

   _____

2. In 1380 _____ made the first translation of the Bible into English.

3. Tyndale's translation was made directly from the _____.

4. Either quote or give the substance of Tyndale's prayer at the stake. ⸺⸺⸺⸺⸺⸺⸺⸺⸺

⸺⸺⸺⸺⸺⸺⸺⸺⸺⸺⸺⸺

5. What two names are given to the translation which was completed in 1611? ⸺⸺⸺⸺ or ⸺⸺⸺⸺.

6. What is the most important principle for a translator to observe? ⸺⸺⸺⸺⸺⸺⸺⸺⸺

7. Do you have a modern version that particularly speaks to you? If so, can you explain why? ⸺⸺⸺⸺

⸺⸺⸺⸺⸺⸺⸺⸺⸺⸺⸺⸺

⸺⸺⸺⸺⸺⸺⸺⸺⸺⸺⸺⸺

8. Can you explain why the King James Version has been the favorite for so many centuries? ⸺⸺⸺⸺⸺

⸺⸺⸺⸺⸺⸺⸺⸺⸺⸺⸺⸺

⸺⸺⸺⸺⸺⸺⸺⸺⸺⸺⸺⸺

Make This Personal

Memorize 2 Corinthians 4:5-7.

For we preach not ourselves, but Christ Jesus the Lord;
And ourselves your servants for Jesus' sake.

For God, who commanded the light to shine out of darkness, hath shined in our hearts,
To give the light of the knowledge of the glory of God in the face of Jesus Christ.

But we have this treasure in earthen vessels,
That the excellency of the power may be of God, and not of us.

A Further Word

Here in the original Scriptures is something so far above human attainment that a fully adequate translation is well-nigh impossible of achievement. Not one but several versions are needed to bring out anything of the fullness of the simplest New Testament narrative.

When all the heat and dust of controversy as to the 'mechanics' of inspiration have subsided, and when the quibblings of the critics as to who wrote what, are forgotten, the Scriptures will remain the unchanging record of God communicating to His creatures, of Christ revealing Himself to His church.

Herbert Dennett, *A Guide to Modern Versions of the New Testament,* p. vii.

7

How to Understand the Bible

Something for You to Study

Think for a moment about the facts you have studied in these lessons. Which of them would you absolutely have to know to understand the central message of the Bible? Must a person know all the history of the translations in order to be blessed by Psalm 23? Would one have to be able to explain all the theories of inspiration to understand the Christmas story in Luke 2? Would you have to be able to explain in detail how God gave the Bible by inspiration in order to believe John 3:16?

Each of these facts is important in helping us appreciate what a wonderful book the Bible is. But the person who knows nothing at all about them can still be gripped by the Bible's central message—the redemption provided by Christ Jesus which was God's plan from before the creation of the world (see Ephesians 1; 1 Peter 1:18-20). Certain facts are clear to even the casual reader of the Bible. They are as follows:

All men are sinners—Romans 3:23
God provides salvation from sin—Romans 6:23
Salvation is found only in Jesus Christ—Acts 4:12
Salvation is a free gift—Ephesians 2:8-9

On the other hand, the answer to the question Can everything in the Bible be understood is no. Since the Bible is the Word of God—who is all-wise—we should expect to find difficult things in it. If God were not beyond our limited comprehension, He would not be God. This is clearly indicated in Isaiah 55:8-9.

48

The Bible distinguishes between the world's wisdom and God's wisdom. The wisdom of the world is humanistic, glorifying man rather than God. The wisdom of God is supernatural and divine and centers in Jesus Christ. Therefore all our education should be integrated with the Scriptures which reveal God. We should not think it necessary to revise the Bible every time a new theory is advanced in education. In all our study we should subordinate everything to the question "What saith the Scripture?" In it is found the wisdom of God. It sometimes takes man's knowledge a long time to appreciate God's wisdom.

Having given His Word in such a marvelous way and preserved it so wonderfully down through the centuries, God has not left it a closed, incomprehensible Book. He has equally marvelously provided that it can be understood through the teaching of the Holy Spirit. Whenever we do not understand something in the Bible, we can ask help from the Holy Spirit who knows the answer to every question.

The Holy Spirit, who indwells everyone who believes in Christ, enlarges the capacity for understanding spiritual truth (see John 16:13). He shows the simple things of Scripture first. He tells us that God is love and that He made us and loves us. Then He goes on to explain just how great God's power and majesty and love are.

First Corinthians 2:14 indicates that spiritual truth cannot be understood by men without the illuminating ministry of the Holy Spirit. This doesn't mean that no part of God's Word can be understood by those who are not yielded to God. The Bible can be read from an historical background, for example, and be comprehensible even to a person who is not a Christian. The account of the life and death of the Lord Jesus can be read and appreciated even by one who does not accept Him as Saviour. But a spiritual interpretation of the truths of God in the Bible is given only by the Holy Spirit.

As we read the Bible under the guidance of the Holy Spirit, we find that there is work involved in studying it. The meaning of the Bible is discovered by a careful study of its words, phrases, paragraphs, sections, and books. To really interpret the Bible correctly we must know its central theme and purpose, the relationship of each book to the others, the specific theme of the individual books, and the literary form of the books. Many people have only a limited knowledge of the Bible because they have been exposed only to a chapter here, a section there, a few verses in another place. No passage of Scripture should be interpreted apart from its context or setting. This is a common-sense rule that is often disregarded.

All of this requires work, but it is work that is well rewarded in a deeper understanding of God's Word. In studying the Bible one should observe the following:

1. *The purpose of the Bible.* Its purpose is not to teach science or history or geography; its main purpose is to teach about God. The first sentence of the Bible flatly states that He exists. Then it goes on to tell more of what He is like and what He does and what His purpose is for the world. That is why the Bible was written—to reveal God.

2. *The separate message of each book.* Each book has a specific theme. The four Gospels are an example of this. Each was written from a different viewpoint: Matthew shows the Lord Jesus as King; Mark, as Servant; Luke, as Man; John, as God. Knowing that each book has its own message helps explain why some parts of the Bible—Numbers and Chronicles, for example—do not mean as much to us as do Romans or Ephesians.

3. *The context of the message.* It is not wise to lift a verse out of its setting and try to understand what it means. What goes before and what comes after is important to know. A statement made by the devil and quoted in the Bible cannot be introduced by the words "The Bible says."

4. *The complete message is spread throughout the Bible.* The important teachings of the Bible are given in different

places in different books. One gives a part of God's purpose and another gives some more. The Old Testament is an unfinished book; it needs the New Testament. We have the complete picture only when we read it all.

5. *The Bible is great literature.* Sometimes God put the message He wanted to give in poetry form (the Psalms); sometimes the message was a prophecy (Jeremiah). Deep doctrinal truths are found in a letter to a personal friend (Philemon). The Lord Jesus frequently used parables in His teaching. But all of the Bible blends together in one harmonious whole.

Find Out for Yourself

1. Read Jeremiah 15:16. What two words did Jeremiah use to describe the effect God's Word had on him? _____

   _____ and _____ Explain what he meant by eating God's Word. _____

   _____

2. Read John 16:12-14. What adjective is used to describe the Spirit? _____ Make a list of all the things these verses say the Holy Spirit will do.

   _____

   _____

   _____

   _____

   What will He *not* do? _____

3. Read Hebrews 5:12. What are some of the "first principles" of the Word of God found in the following verses?

Romans 3:23 _____

Romans 6:23 _____

Acts 4:12 _____

Ephesians 2:8-9 _____

4. What "strong meat" do the following verses contain?

Colossians 3:1-2 _____

_____

Ephesians 6:13 _____

_____

1 Corinthians 13 _____

2 Peter 3:17-18 _____

_____

Check Your Memory

Without looking back at the study material answer these questions.

1. The message of the Bible centers in _____.

2. We should expect to find difficult things in the Bible be-cause _____.

3. What is indicated in Isaiah 55:8-9? _____

_____

4. John 16:13 tells the work of the Holy Spirit. What is it?

_____

5. The purpose of the Bible is to _____.

6. What would you say is the difference between reading the **Bible and studying the Bible?** _____

Make This Personal

Memorize Psalm 119:97-104.

> O how love I thy law!
> It is my meditation all the day.

> Thou through thy commandments hast made me wiser than
> mine enemies:
> For they are ever with me.

> I have more understanding than all my teachers:
> For thy testimonies are my meditation.

> I understand more than the ancients,
> Because I keep thy precepts.

> I have refrained my feet from every evil way,
> That I might keep thy word.

> I have not departed from thy judgments:
> For thou hast taught me.

> How sweet are thy words unto my taste!
> Yea, sweeter than honey to my mouth!

> Through thy precepts I get understanding:
> Therefore I hate every false way.

A Further Word

The God of Scripture is revealed as a God of purpose, a God of sovereignty, a God who has not disclosed everything, but a God who has provided the materials and substance for a faith that is intelligent. The Scriptures, therefore, record what God has done in the past as He has dealt with sin and human failure. The Scriptures affirm the promises of God, the certainty of their fulfillment, whether predictions of grace or judgment. The Scriptures reveal the providence of God in His sovereignty, even in a world that is confused, sinful, and rebellious. The Scriptures reveal a purpose moving through the pages of human history. There is no true philosophy of human history except as it is given in Scripture, and the many attempts of men to give meaning to history apart from Scripture are their own refutation. . . .

Students of Scripture, while reveling in the completeness of divine revelation, nevertheless must confess that they know only a fragment of the whole. With Paul they must exclaim: "O the depth of the riches both of the wisdom and knowledge of God! How unsearchable are his judgments, and his ways past finding out! For who hath known the mind of the Lord? or who hath been his counsellor?" (Romans 11:33-34).

John F. Walvoord, "The Hope of the World," in *The Word for This Century,* ed. Merrill C. Tenney, pp. 159-60. Reprinted by permission of the publisher, Oxford University Press, Inc.

8

How to Study the Bible

Something for You to Study

A bank teller does not have to study every possible kind of counterfeit money in order to recognize bogus bills. Actually he couldn't possibly be familiar with them all. But he can recognize a counterfeit bill if he knows what the real one looks like. The better he knows the real, the more expert he will be in detecting the false.

This is one of the main reasons for studying the Bible. Paul admonishes us not to be "tossed to and fro, and carried about with every wind of doctrine" (Ephesians 4:14). The person who does not know the Bible will be at the mercy of every cultist who comes along. False teachers can and do use the Bible. They frequently quote from it and refer to it in support of their false or peculiar beliefs. The one who is grounded in God's Word will not be swayed by teaching that is falsely based on the Bible.

But the primary reason for studying the Bible should be a consuming desire to know God better. It is He who is revealed throughout its pages, and only through knowing His Word will we know Him.

The most obvious Bible study method—and the one most often overlooked because it is so obvious—is to read the Bible itself. It must *all* be read, not just the same bits over and over. Reading an entire book through at one sitting enables one to see its message more readily than by reading a chapter now and then or a few verses occasionally. Years ago Dr. James M. Gray in his book *How to Master the English Bible* developed the idea that one must have a knowledge of the factual content of the Bible before he can study it properly. This knowledge comes through reading the Bible itself, for the Bible is its own best commentary.

The books themselves sometimes give information that can be learned by a simple reading. Many of them easily answer the question What's in this book? Even Revelation gives answers in the opening verses to questions concerning the author, the receiver, and ₜthe theme. The salutations and concluding verses of the epistles often identify people, places, and sometimes purposes.

However, one should also make use of whatever helps are available in commentaries, Bible dictionaries, and other books. No one needs to be completely independent in his study of the Bible. Each student of the Word can build upon and add to the efforts of godly Bible scholars who have gone before him. Every Bible student has a wealth of material available in inexpensive form. The Moody Correspondence School offers a variety of courses from an easily understood survey of the Scriptures to more detailed Bible study.

Three basic questions we should always ask as we begin the study of a book in the Bible should be applied in the following order of importance:

What does it say? *This is observation.*
What does it mean? *This is interpretation.*
What does it mean to me? *This is application.*

There are many, many different methods that can be used to study the Bible, but space permits only a brief survey of a few of them.

Book Study

The purpose of this method is to find the overall structure and meaning of the book. This can be done by first noting the main divisions of a book. Galatians' broad outlines can be set up as follows:

Chapters					
1	2	3	4	5	6
Personal Explanation		Doctrinal Exposition		Practical Application	

In book study, one should try to see the relationships within the book. Here a chart is helpful, as in this study of Job.

Chapters									
1	2	3		31	32	37	38	41	42
	P R O B L E M	Dialogue — Argument— false philosophy Eliphaz, Bildad, Zophar			Elihu speaks		Jehovah speaks	S O L U T I O N	Epilogue after the testing
Prologue before the testing									
		Job Answers							

In studying a book of the Bible it is important also to note the relationship of one book to another. For example, the closing words of Genesis are a preparation for what is to come in the next book.

"God will . . . bring you out of this land." → "And the LORD said, . . . I am come down to deliver."

Genesis 50:24   Exodus 3:7-8

GEOGRAPHICAL STUDY

Geography is important in Bible study, for often the mention of places gives a clue to the message of a book. In Hebrews 11:8 we read: "By faith Abraham . . . went out, not knowing whither he went." This is used as an illustration of faith. Why?

We turn back to Genesis 11:31 to see why Abraham is important in the record in the New Testament. The rest of Genesis and the remainder of the story of the Bible is concerned in various ways with this land into which Abraham went by faith.

BIOGRAPHICAL STUDY

This is a valuable method of understanding the Bible, for the Bible is a record of people in relation to God. The Bible is the story of the whole human race. It is the story of the Jewish nation, and in the New Testament it is also the story of the church. But these stories center around individuals, and studying them makes the Bible come alive in a special way.

TOPICAL STUDY

This is simply tracing a certain subject by finding all that the Bible has to say about it. Sometimes such a study takes one through the entire Bible. The prophecies of the coming of Christ are an example, beginning as they do with the first general reference in Genesis 3 and continuing through the Bible, becoming more numerous and more specific.

These are only a few of the kinds of study which will give an insight into God's Word. Real, earnest Bible study, however, can benefit only a Christian. The Word clearly states that the things of God are foolishness to the one who does not believe and, conversely, that they can be known only by the one who is spiritual (1 Corinthians 2:14-15).

We must come to Bible study—

prayerfully;

willing to let God teach;

using helps when needed, including a study Bible, a concordance, a Bible dictionary, a Bible atlas, several modern versions, several commentaries;

with the knowledge of having started down a road that will not end until He who is the central figure of the Word is seen face to face.

Find Out for Yourself

1. Read Deuteronomy 6:6-7. What specific times are mentioned as being appropriate for thinking of God's Word?

   _____

   _____

   _____

   _____

2. What will a knowledge of the Word of God do for us according to the following Scriptures?

   1 Peter 2:2 _____

   Psalm 119:98-99 _____

   2 Timothy 3:15 _____

   Jeremiah 15:16 _____

   Psalm 119:9 _____

3. Read Ephesians through at one sitting. Then go through it again and try to chart its divisions by chapters.

1	6

4. Did you notice how the doctrinal and practical portions intermingle? Reread 5:1-4 and 18-33. Which of these verses contain the doctrinal teaching? Which the practical application?

	Verses 1-4	Verses 18-33
Doctrine	_____	_____
Practical application	_____	_____

Check Your Memory

Without looking back at the study material answer these questions.

1. The simplest way of knowing what the Bible says is to

   _____.

2. The most important reason for studying the Bible is _____

   _____.

3. What are the three basic questions to ask in Bible study?

   _____ which is observation.

   _____ which is _____.

   _____ which is _____.

4. What are the main divisions of Galatians?

   _____ in chapters _____.

   _____ in chapters _____.

   _____ in chapters _____.

5. Who are the only people who can understand spiritual truths? _____

Make This Personal

Memorize James 1:22-25.

> But be ye doers of the word,
> And not hearers only, deceiving your own selves.
>
> For if any be a hearer of the word, and not a doer,
> He is like unto a man beholding his natural face in a glass.
>
> For he beholdeth himself, and goeth his way,
> And straightway forgetteth what manner of man he was.
>
> But whoso looketh into the perfect law of liberty, and continueth therein,
> He being not a forgetful hearer, but a doer of the work,
> This man shall be blessed in his deed.

A Further Word

Spirituality and Bible study in the Christian church go hand in hand. Spirituality cannot be driven into a man, for it involves hunger. The church may invite the Christian to the spiritual banquet, offer a well-balanced and wholesome menu, provide attractive atmosphere and efficient service; but if the man is not hungry he will not eat. In physical hunger, the body wonderfully knows its need, and so craves food. For spiritual hunger, the Christian must know he is in need. He must know that he needs to grow in grace, to please his Saviour, to be aware of the demands of the Word, to know what his heritage is in Christ, to appropriate the strength and power which God offers, to recognize the devices of Satan, and to interpret the times in which he lives. If the Christian knows these are among his greatest needs and that the Bible not only identifies these needs but also meets them, he will hunger for this Word. There is no abnormality about being a serious Bible student. In God's eyes it is most normal because it is most necessary.

Irving L. Jensen, *Independent Bible Study,* pp. 17-18.

Moody Press, a ministry of the Moody Bible Institute, is designed for education, evangelization and edification. If we may assist you in knowing more about Christ and the Christian life, please write us without obligation to: Moody Press, c/o MLM, Chicago, Illinois 60610.

For Further Study

Archer, Gleason L. *A Survey of Old Testament Introduction*. Chicago: Moody, 1964.

Barker, Glenn W.; Lane, William L.; and Michaels, J. Ramsey. *The New Testament Speaks*. New York: Harper & Row, 1969.

Bruce, F. F. *Second Thoughts on the Dead Sea Scrolls*. Grand Rapids: Eerdmans, 1956.

————. *The Books and the Parchments*. New York: Revell, 1963.

————. *The English Bible*. New York: Oxford U., 1961.

Dennett, Herbert. *A Guide to Modern Versions of the New Testament*. Chicago: Moody, 1966.

Gaussen, L. *The Inspiration of the Holy Scriptures*. Chicago: Moody, 1940.

Harris, R. Laird. *The Inspiration and Canonicity of the Bible*. Grand Rapids: Zondervan, 1957.

Henry, Carl F. H., ed. *Revelation and the Bible*. Philadelphia: Presb. & Ref., 1958.

Jensen, Irving L. *Independent Bible Study*. Chicago: Moody, 1963.

Lightfoot, Neil R. *How We Got the Bible*. Grand Rapids: Baker, 1963.

Pfeiffer, Charles F. *Between the Testaments*. Grand Rapids: Baker, 1959.

Price, Ira. *The Ancestry of Our English Bible*. New York: Harper & Row, 1949.

Tenney, Merrill C., ed. *The Word for This Century*. New York: Oxford U., 1960.

Vos, Howard. *Effective Bible Study*. 2d ed. Grand Rapids: Zondervan, 1956.

Walvoord, John F., ed. *Inspiration and Interpretation*. Grand Rapids: Eerdmans, 1957.

Notes